FOUR LAMBS OF AHMICI

A One Act Play By
Antony Jenkins

APS Books,
4 Oakleigh Road,
Stourbridge,
West Midlands,
DY8 2JX

APS Books is a subsidiary of the APS Publications imprint

www.andrewsparke.com

First published worldwide by APS Books in 2019

A catalogue record for this book is available from the British Library

Set against the backdrop of the Bosnian War, Four Lambs of Ahmiči tells the story of four people awaiting rescue from NATO. As the Croatian and Serbian forces close In around them, a single U.N soldier must keep the peace between three Survivors, one of which has a deadly secret.

Four Lambs of Ahmiči was first Performed in 2014 at Hereford's Courtyard Centre for the Arts as Part of the England Drama Festival With the following cast:

U.N- Ian Smith.
Old Man- David Thomas.
Nurse- Katy Dalton.
Man- William Moore

Directed by Anthony Jenkins
Sound Richard Loveridge
Lighting Sue Grenfell

Characters

U.N-	A British soldier in his mid-30s.
Old man-	A Serbian civilian in his late-60s.
Nurse-	A Croatian Nurse in her mid-20s.
Man-	A Bosniak soldier in his late teens.

A derelict house in Ahmiči, Bosnia, September 1992.

A tuning wireless crackles followed by a cacophony of ITN and BBC news reports about the conflict.

Lights begin to flicker as a *bombardment begins. Suddenly a young girl dashes into the house followed by a soldier dragging a wounded man. An older man limps behind after them. After a few moments the bombing dies down but continues faintly throughout the piece. The soldier ransacks through the house ripping down curtains to make blankets. The Old man turns and stands in the doorway staring out.*

U.N- (*To the old man*) No! No! Away! Stay away!

He escorts the Old Man away from the door. Suddenly a voice calls out on the U.N radio.

V/O- **'Alpha 4?! Alpha One-Zero, do you copy over?'**

U.N- Alpha One-Zero...this is Alpha 4 receiving you, over!

V/O- **'…Reports of heavy fire in your area...What is your SITREP …over'.**

U.N- Alpha One-Zero, SITREP is some bastard starting shelling as soon as the evacuation began! (*Wiping the sweat and trickle of blood from his forehead*) Transport's gone, we're scattered all over the place and the losses are many! I'm held up in a shack about half a mile south of the extraction point. I've got one man down, unresponsive. I've also two others, they're pretty beaten up but they're ok, request immediate pick up, over

V/O- **'…Alpha 4, we advise you stay where you are! The Serbs have dug into the mountains to the west of you and are targeting civilian areas in the south!'**

U.N- (To himself) Christ!

V/O- **'…we can't risk a rescue at this time! Two patrols are pinned down in Bradina and Bosnian**

roadblocks are slowing down our convoys in Vitez! Major Lewis and the battalion are on their way to Ahmiči to organise a cease fire, he'll pick you up on the way back. Acknowledge so far, over'.

U.N- Alpha One-Zero I acknowledge, but what of the wounded?! Over!

V/O- **'…Alpha 4, just do the best you can at this time! Good luck, Alpha One-Zero out.**

U.N- (*To himself*) Fuckin' 'ell! (*Composes himself*) Ok…ok…does anyone speak English? (*They all stare*) Engleski? Anyone? Does anyone understand?

Nurse- Yes, I understand you.

U.N- Good! Ok, look my commander, my boss is gonna find whoever's bombing the place and get 'em to stop firing so we can...

Old man- Nije srpski!

U.N- …what? What did you say?

Old man- I heard you boy, it's not Serbians! It's not us U.N! It's those fucking murdering Croat pigs!

U.N- Hang on a second, you heard what…

Old man- Sranjé! Look around you! It is them I am telling you! Croats! Bastards! (*Indicating to outside*) Look what they're doing! Look what they're doing to the place! They've taken the hills and now they want the city! They're responsible for this (*screams to the outside world*) murdering bastards!

U.N- Listen to me! (*Approaching him reassuringly*) I need you to calm down, ok?! Relax, take a breath! Just wait for…

Old man- (*Shaking him off*) I cannot wait U.N! I've got to get out of here. I must get home!

U.N- (*Steps in front*) I cannot allow that!

Old man- What?! What do you mean 'you cannot allow'?!

U.N- I cannot allow any of you to leave right now its suicide! Listen to it out there!

Old man- This is my home U.N you've no right to order me!

U.N- I'm not ordering…

Old man- No right to come to my home and tell me when and where I can go!

U.N- Listen to me, anyone who sets one foot out of here is dead do you understand me?! You speak English I'm sure you understand that word 'dead'! Yes?

Old man- Fuck you U.N! My family needs me!

U.N- You're family will see you again I promise! Just calm down!

Old man- (*Scoffs*) they could all be dead for all you know!

U.N- You don't know that mate...

Old man- I am not your mate!

U.N- Ok look, I give you my word your family are safe. Just wait until help arrives and we'll take you to them.

Old man- Jebi Se U.N!

The Old man heads for the door the U.N steps in front of him again, there's a struggle and the U.N pushes the Old Man back inside the house.

U.N- You're not going anywhere!

Old man- I am not a prisoner!

U.N- Shut up and listen! You walk out of here your family will never see you again! Get it?

Old man- I am Serbian boy! I'm safer than any of you!

The U.N stands firm and the old man

steps back.

U.N- You're safer with me pal, I suggest you accept that.

Old Man chuckles and walks away mumbling to himself.

Nurse- When will your commander come?

U.N- Soon. Here.

He offers cigarettes.

Nurse- I'm sorry I don't.

U.N offers a cigarette to the old man who takes the whole packet and sits in his corner. The U.N stares in disbelief.

Old man- What? You think a packet of cigarettes will make this any easier? Ha!

U.N- I'm so sorry this has happened to you, to all of you, but we're here and I will not let anything happen to you so long as you co-operate with me…yes?

Old man- Sranje! You have promised many things in the past

U.N.

Nurse- We would be dead if it wasn't for him.

Old man- Who asked you?!

U.N- That's enough! Look, I'm in the same boat as you. I know how you feel, I wanna be back home with my feet up like the rest of you! But I can't, so make your peace with it.

U.N checks on the wounded man.

Old man- You are like us?

U.N- What?

Old man- You say you are like us?

U.N- I'm in the same boat yes.

Old man- Then you have no authority over me U.N! You are another refugee in a room. You're nothing!

U.N- Look, enough of this shit! I'm here to help you and keep you from getting your fucking head blown off! You see this? It says 'United Nations', peacekeepers, understand?

Old man chuckles and sarcastically applauds.

Old man- You're doing well U.N (!)

U.N- (*Quietly face to face*) Listen to me pal, you're in here alive and well because of us, because of me. Surely a little courtesy wouldn't go a miss 'mate'?! And even if you can't extend that courtesy how about you shut your trap for a bit before I shut it for you, eh?

The U.N turns and assists the nurse. The distant gunfire continues to crackle.

Old man- You don't understand 'boy' this is my land, my home! I am free to go wherever I want!

U.N- Excuse me, but haven't you noticed the shit that's going on lately?! You bastards are killing each other on a daily basis all because of 'your land!' Snipers will just as easily kill you as they would me or her.

Old man- Croats would they don't care! Or Muslim. Soulless bastards!

U.N- The world sees differently.

Old man- The world doesn't care U.N.

U.N- I'm living proof that it does!

Old man laughs.

Old man- You?! (*Chuckles*) Bosnia calls for help and they send blue helmets and paperwork! You cannot fight you cannot shoot! You cannot do anything! They should have sent boy scouts instead.

U.N- Our mandate is to shelter and protect.

Old man- (*Chuckles*) you did well in Srebrenica! Isn't that right, U.N? Marched out by its' own people! When will you understand boy, you are not wanted here! Go! Leave! Leaves us in peace! We can end this without your help!

U.N- Markale Market ring any bells? Hm? Remember that? Sixty people dead and fuck knows how many injured thanks to your Serb brothers! Hundreds came running up to us with that look in their eyes, wondering 'why?' 'Why is this happening?' 'What had they done to deserve this?' I tell you now pal, having a six-year-old asking why I'm sticking what's left of his mother in a bin bag is something the likes of you will never understand!

Old man- That was Muslim shelling Muslim!

U.N- Bullshit! Serb Generals even boasted about it!

Old man- Don't believe everything you see in the media boy! Muslims are far worse! And Croats? Well, they eat their own.

U.N- Bloody delusional propaganda.

Old man grabs some dirt off the floor.

Old man- Look...Serbian soil! Look U.N!

U.N- (*Rifling through his bergen*) I'm dealing with other important matters at the moment.

Old man- (*Gripping the dirt*) Serbian land. My land. We kill all who threaten to defile it. We fight to save ourselves!

U.N doesn't answer.

Old man- …UN?!

U.N- How the fuck can a 6-year-old defile your land?! Huh?! There's no logic or reasoning behind your bloody brutality! Serbian or otherwise! Fucking beheadings and child rapings it's all lunacy! Barbaric!

Old man- We've been doing it for centuries U.N, all the blue helmets in the world cannot stop it.

U.N- We can try.

Old man- That's all you do boy is try! You cannot stop a nation defending itself.

U.N- Jesus, give it a rest would you?

Old man- Do you believe we Serbs will simply step aside and let Croatian pigs take our homes?! What would you do boy, huh? (*U.N doesn't answer*) You know I am right, don't you boy? You know I speak the truth. And that boy would have grown up to be like his father and we would be dragged back into this shit again. History repeating history.

The old man finds a stool and slumps in a corner away from the others. He draws a line in the dirt.

Old man- My land.

The awkward silence is suddenly broken by the nurse.

Nurse- Thank you. Thank you for being here.

U.N- You're welcome.

Nurse- You're very kind. Like Noah and this is your ark.

U.N- More like a knackered canoe. How is he?

Nurse- I think some of his ribs are broken, his right is broken, some deep cuts in both legs and he has a severe head wound. He's lucky to be alive.

Old man- You call that lucky?

Nurse- I've done all that I can, but he needs morphine.

U.N- He's had my last shot, there's nothing else I can give him.

Nurse- We must get him to a hospital.

Old man- He's finished U.N. There's nothing left of him, put him out of his misery.

Nurse- Please don't say that!

U.N- Pay no attention to him. What's your name?

Nurse- Maria Kadic.

U.N- Ok Maria, I want you to…

Old man- 'Kadic'?

U.N- …keep him warm and make sure he doesn't loose any more blood…

Old man- 'Kadic'?!

U.N- …you seem to have a magic touch you're doing well.

Old man- Did you say 'Kadic'?

Nurse- Yes, I'm a nurse at the hospital.

Old man- 'Kadic' Croatian? No?

U.N- She's a nurse that's all that matters here!

Old man- You're a Croat? Kadic?!

Nurse- I am.

U.N- So what?

Old man- She's the reason we're here U.N! Throw her out!

Let snipers deal with her!

U.N steps in front of him.

U.N- Don't start that shit again!

Old man- You and I are in here because of her! She's probably a spy!

Nurse- Please, I'm not a spy!

Old man- She's a traitor U.N! She'll throw us to the wolves!

Nurse- It's not true…

Old man- We'll be carried out of here! She'll call her bastards down and they'll kill us all!

Nurse- No I…

Old man- She probably signalled to them to start shooting at us!

U.N- For God sake she's not a spy, she's a civilian like you!

Old man- Fuck her! She's nothing like me! Throw the bitch

out!

U.N- What's happening here is not her fault!

Nurse- Please believe me sir! I'm not a spy!

Old man- Shut your mouth bitch! This is your doing! This is your fault!

He attacks her, the U.N intervenes and pins him against the wall.

U.N- Don't you touch her!

Old man- On her side U.N?!

U.N- I'm on no one's side.

Old man- (*Spits at him*) Traitor!

U.N- Shut up and listen to me! None of this is her fault. And as far as I'm concerned, she's keeping this boy alive. One more false move out of you and I won't be so civil, do you understand me?!

Old Man- Izdajnik! You favour Croat whores U.N? You like little pigs? Go, take her side boy, but I warn you, you will suffer for this!

The Old Man makes a vulgar gesture, shrugs off the U.N and goes back to his corner again.

U.N- Look, I get there isn't any trust left in this country, God knows I'll never know the reasons behind it all. But try to understand that I'm trying to help you here, all of you. Can we all be at peace for a moment? Hm? Whiskey?

U.N pulls out a hip flask.

U.N- Bells. Good stuff.

U.N pours some into a tin cup and hands it to the old man, who after a moment of hesitation takes a huge swig.

U.N- Lovely stuff isn't it?

Old man spits.

Old man- It's piss!

U.N- This is all I drink back in England…my home in a bottle.

He offers the nurse she declines.

U.N- Look, I know things look like shit, but I promise you both its only for a short time. Mint?

Offers her a mint.

Nurse- No thank you.

U.N- I'm afraid I've nothing in the way of food.

Nurse- I'm not hungry.

U.N- How long have you been a nurse Maria?

Nurse- Two years, I graduated before the war started and have worked in the hospital since. I also assist the Red Cross.

U.N- Got any family?

Nurse- Yes *(Pulling out a photograph*) my Mother Maria, I'm named after her, my father Raif he's a doctor…and my brother...Tomas.

U.N- He a doctor too?

Nurse- ...A soldier.

Old man grunts in disgust.

Nurse- He’s only 16 a medic for the HOS. A very gentle soul. Beautiful boy. We haven’t heard from him in some months, he wrote us every day then suddenly…nothing. In our church we pray and light candles each day for him. Every morning my father walks to the top of a hill behind our house and calls out to him…but there’s no reply.

U.N- When this is all over you’ll have your Tomas back safe and sound, I’m sure of it.

Nurse- Thank you.

Old man- Sad, sad, sight.

U.N- What now?

Old man- It’s bad enough you talk to her but to lie to so sweetly is cruel U.N.

U.N- I’m giving her hope.

Old man- He’s probably dead in a ditch like most Croats.

U.N- You don’t know that.

Old man- And you do? You don’t even know where you are. How could you possibly know where he is?

U.N- Don’t listen to him Maria, your brother is fine I’m sure.

Nurse- How do you know?

U.N- …well…

The radio screeches to life.

V/O- **‘Alpha 4, Alpha One-Zero, are you receiving over?’**

U.N- Thank god! This is Alpha 4 receiving…go ahead over.

V/O- **‘…Major Lewis is unable to reach you at this time. The roadblocks in your area are too dangerous for our convoys and the local militia will not cooperate! Acknowledge so far,**

over'.

U.N- ((To himself) Jesus! Alpha One-Zero, I acknowledge but I'm need of medical assistance, surely the Major can spare somebody?! Over.

V/O- **'...Alpha 4, you must understand that right now we're flying blind! Safe zones no longer correspond with any of our maps and casualties on our side are increasing! Major Lewis is still in the process of locating the Serbian and Croat Generals to organise this ceasefire to get you out, but you have to be patient! We're spread too thin on the ground to assist all patrols! Just keep your head down and we'll be with you ASAP! Alpha One-Zero, out.**

U.N- Bastards!

Silence (apart from the distant shelling).

Old man- You are going to create a lot of paperwork boy.

U.N- Bloody cowards! Bunch of cock sucking wankers! Call 'em selves soldiers?!

Old man- There is no room for heroes boy, not in Amici!

U.N- Shut up.

Nurse- So...we wait here?

Old man- You can. I know other ways home.

Nurse- He won't last long U.N he needs a hospital!

Old man- Put him out of his suffering. He won't feel anything.

Nurse- Please don't say such things, he's just a boy!

Old man- He's as good as dead U.N leave him.

Nurse- NO! You can't leave him U.N! Please!

Old man- Let's take care of the living for now boy, yes?

Nurse- What shall we do? (*No answer*) U.N? What should we do?

U.N- You heard my orders. We wait.

Nurse- But he'll die if we don't get him…

U.N- I KNOW!! I know the situation! But what can I do?! If we leave here we're all fucked! (*Pause*) No, we wait here for a patrol, that's our best chance, there aren't any other options!

Old man- Nightfall, that is my option.

U.N- Yeah? Then what? Fondle your way through bushes and razor wire and HOPE you don't step on a land mine?! What's your plan for running into Croatian hands, hmm? What's your 'plan' to prevent your head ending up on a fucking flagpole?

Old man- All risks I'm willing to take.

U.N- Then go! Just go! I'm tired of this! I've tried to make you realise what's happening out there but you're either to fucking dumb or stubborn to see sense! If either of you want to go, then go! Piss off! And best of luck to you.

Silence.

Nurse- I want to stay. Please.

U.N- Well as Gandhi over there pointed out I've no authority here, so you're free to do whatever you want.

He heads to the doorway and stares out. Pause.

Nurse- '*Fear not, for I am with you; be not dismayed, I will strengthen you, I will help you, I will uphold you with my righteous right hand*'. My mother often recites comforting words like that. Does that comfort you?

U.N- Not really. But thank you for the effort.

U.N rifles through and checks his limited supplies. The old man rummages around the drawers and empty cases.

U.N- Oi! I hope you're not looting?

Old man- Loot? What am I going to loot? The walls? Relax boy you worry too much. Find your peace.

The old man finds an old radio.

Old man- Ah! Some good after all! I promise I won't 'loot' it.

He then sits on his stool and switches it on. He tunes through the static until he hears an angelic folk song. For a moment the distant shelling is drowned out by the music and all is at peace. After a few moments the tune cuts out. EXPLOSION! Suddenly the boy gasps and comes too. U.N assists the nurse.

U.N- Easy kid! You're ok! You're in safe hands. Don't move! Lay still!

He coughs violently and winces in pain.

U.N- You're ok, you're safe. Breathe kid, breathe, shhhh.

Nurse- *Govoris Li Engleski? Croat? Huh? Croat?*

U.N- English? Can you understand us?

Man- (*Gasping*) Yes…W…What…what hap…?

U.N- It's ok you're alright you're safe now.

The man tries to move and grunts in pain.

Nurse- Please try not to move.

Man- Who, who, who are you?

U.N- It's ok, just relax. This is Maria she's been looking after you since we got here.

Man- W…where?

U.N- We're in Ahmici, somewhere. We're waiting for my guys to come and take us home.

Old man- Yeah sure (!)

U.N- They're coming! What's your name mate?

Man- R…Rah…Rahmo J…Jamil.

Old man- Bosniak?

Man- Y…Yes.

Old man- (*Chuckling and applauds*) Oh U.N you have a full house!

U.N- Shut up!

Old man- You've the whole country in one room U.N. Let's see if you can do better than NATO.

U.N- That's enough!

Man doesn't answer he's in too much pain.

U.N- You're a civilian yes?

Old man- Or a spy?!

U.N- Will you shut up?!

Man- Min fadlik…please my head I cannot…

Old man- I agree with the boy, you bark too much U.N.

U.N- Just piss off back to your corner!

Old man- More snakes in the room U.N. Be warned.

Nurse- Please! Can I suggest that we should relax a little now? The boy is awake and we're all alive! We should thank God for this.

Old man- Oh yes thank God (!) Praise God (!) Praise him for putting us all in this shit in the first place!

Nurse- God is with us I know it!

Old man- How do you know? Can you see him?!

Nurse- He bought you here safely.

Old man- YOU bought me here you crazy bitch! You're not God! There is no God!

Nurse- I tell you, he saved us!

Old man- He no longer cares! He has forgotten us!

Nurse- He's watching over us, even you.

Old man- Yeah sure (!) You positive we cannot throw her out?!

U.N- That's enough!

Man- Min yatruk…Min…I must go, I must leave (*Grunts in pain*)

U.N- No, no, no stay still! Don't move! Ok, Maria is going to watch over you.

Nurse- Where are you going?

U.N- I'm making a call and getting everyone out of here. This changes everything!

Man- La! No! Please…

He tries to rear up but is paralysed by the pain and is immediately cradled by Maria.

Nurse- You must lie still. Are you sure you can't give him anything?

U.N- I told you I've nothing left. Just keep him warm and try not to excite him.

The man begins to cry in pain. U.N attempts to make a call but the signal has gone.

Nurse- Shhh, its ok I am with you. God is with you.

She continues to wipe his brow and make him more comfortable.

Nurse- (*Prays quietly*) *Heavenly Father I pray you take this boys pain away and let him rest in peace, for he has been wounded by those who have strayed, I pray you send comfort and serenity...*

Old man- Ohh stop your tongue Croat, please.

Nurse- *...This I ask in the name of the father, the son and the Holy Ghost, amen.*

Old man- (*Dropping to his knees*) Oh God, oh merciful, all loving, almighty God I pray, no, I BEG that you shut this woman up! For she is driving your flock insane…

Silence.

Old man- (*Surprised*) Thank you (!)

U.N- Shit! (*Thinking frantically*)

Nurse- What is it?

U.N- The signal is too weak to make proper contact.

Nurse- But you spoke to your men, we heard you.

U.N- Signals come and go. Most of the time it's just guess work.

Nurse- What do we do?

U.N- (*Indicates to the outside world*) gotta stick my head out there. It's our best chance.

Nurse- But what you said about snipers? They could shoot you.

U.N- There's enough cover out there, should be fine. Besides, if I don't make it back you're free to do whatever you want. (*Looks at the Old Man*) aren't ya? I'll be right back.

He leaves.

Old man- Arrogant foolish boy! Budala! You know, if I were dying and you were whining, I'd beg God to take me.

Nurse- All I have left is hope and faith what's wrong with that?

Old man- You're wailing brings nothing.

Nurse- It brings me peace.

Old man- You're too loud with it! And you spit it like a snake!

Nurse- If I could climb the tallest spire and scream to him I would.

Old man- Why don't you try it? You'd make an easy target.

Old man grunts.

Nurse- I have never met you before and yet you talk

to me with spite. Why is that? Do I look like a soldier? Do I look like I could hurt an old man like you? No…I have been taught to love and to cherish. That is me. That is who I am. You'll never change that. You'll never change me.

Old man- Nor me.

Nurse- Then why do you tell me to 'stop praying' and to 'stop believing' when you know I'll never listen?! There are hundreds, thousands like me still holding onto hope.

Old man- You're fools to think some angel will float down and save you. Madness! It's nothing personal, although I cannot stomach the sight of you.

Nurse- I almost feel sorry for you.

Old man- Don't.

Nurse- Why are you such an angry man?

Old man- Angry because I'm trapped in this house with you! I should be at home! I should be with my family! Not in here listening to YOU! FUCK YOU!

Nurse- Ok I'm sorry! Please don't be angry I was just trying to make you see I'm not your enemy. I didn't mean to upset you I'm sorry.

She goes to touch him. He backs away.

Old man- When will you learn that help from heaven never comes, girl?

Nurse- You sound so sure of that.

Old man- Why am I talking to you? I don't know you you are nothing to me so why am I still in the same room talking to you?!

Nurse- Because I am listening. That's how it works isn't it? You talk I listen.

Old man is (for once) speechless.

Nurse- (*Softly*) Can I ask...why are you so certain? Why are you so sure help will never come?

Old man sits quietly for a moment.

Old man- Croat (*Pause*) girl. God supports the wicked, history has shown us that. You see it even today.

Nurse- Not always.

Old man- We had a Croat neighbour by the name of Gideon, he was a priest and a teacher, everyone loved him and attended every service. And in 1944 he threw it all away to save his own skin. Sunday morning came, we flocked to his church eager to hear 'the word of God' but instead we were met by the Ustasi. (*He takes a moment*) Gideon stood at his pulpit and read out every name every creed. And he watched as those named were herded onto trucks like sheep. I saw my entire neighbourhood die in the house of God. I watched my mother and father kneel at Gideon's feet, arms stretched pleading to him, pleading to spare us, pleading to God. I tell you girl, there was no answer that day, no floating angel, no mercy, instead they were met with rifle butts (*Pause*) once the segregation was over, Gideon was also thrown onto a truck. They all went to the same place this I'm certain (*Pause*) Jasenovac. I along with two others were saved because we were strong and able. (*Chuckles to himself briefly*) so let me ask you this girl if a million people didn't get an answer, what chance do you think you have?

Nurse- I'll never stop trying.

Old man walks up to her and kneels next to her.

Old man- Give up girl. Man is the only true God.

As he gets up he spots the watch on Rahmo's wrist.

Old man- You know you can spot a Bosniak pig a mile off? By his jewellery. Cheap, loud shit.

Nurse gently takes the wrist and inspects the watch.

Nurse- My Tomas had a watch like this.

Old man- Your Tomas had no taste.

U.N enters. Nurse continues to inspect the watch.

U.N- Ok, good news! From what I could make out both Croats and Serbs are aware of NATO's presence in Ahmici.

Old man- And yet they still shoot at you?

U.N- Look, they've both agreed to a ceasefire or at least give us some time to evacuate.

Old man- And then what?

U.N- We make for a new safe zone outside Vitez.

Old man- What of me? What of my family?

U.N- We're moving everybody out of Ahmici so you'll meet them in Vitez.

Old man- You are sure?

U.N- I promise.

Old man- How long will it take?

U.N- It's all happening as we speak. Best bloody news I've had all day (!) First thing I'm gonna do is have a brew.

Old man- 'Brew?'

U.N- Yeah brew ya know? Cup of tea.

The conversation is cut short by the nurse staring down at Rahmo.

Nurse- Where is he?! Where is my Tomas? Please tell me Rahmo where is my brother!

U.N- Hey, hey what's wrong?

Nurse- Where is he?!

U.N- What's wrong? Maria what is it?

Nurse- This is my brother's watch!

U.N- What? How can you be sure?

Old man- Plenty of shit like that on the markets.

Nurse- It's his I swear to you! Look…it has his initials on the strap those are his! It's Tomas'! Where is he?!

U.N- Calm down Maria, calm down. (*Gently*) Rahmo? Rahmo can you hear me?

Nurse- (*Frantic*) Wake up please!

U.N- Stand back Maria!

Old man moves her back.

U.N- Rahmo can you hear?!

Rahmo comes too.

U.N- Rahmo…this watch? You see it? Is it yours?

Man- W…what...

U.N- This watch? Is it yours?

Man- Y...yes.

U.N- You are sure Rahmo?

Man- It is mine.

U.N- He says it's his Maria.

Nurse- If that is true then what do these letters mean to you?

Man- Madha, w…what…what letters?

Nurse- These! (*Becoming desperate*) These letters! These letters! 'T.K' what do they mean? What do they mean to you?!

Rahmo groans in pain and mumbles.

Nurse- They're my brother's initials! They're his I swear it! Where did you get his watch Rahmo?! Please? PLEASE!

Man tries to roll away.

Nurse- (*Slamming back down he screams*) Where is my brother?!

Man- 'Idi do djavola' (*He grunts in pain and*

frustration) I want to go.

Nurse- (Shaking him) tell me!

U.N- Hey back off! The boy says it's his! You must be mistaken Maria. I'm sorry.

Nurse- I tell you he knows where he is U.N! Believe me, I tell you he knows!

U.N- Maria look at him, the kid hasn't a clue what day it is! Look, I understand you're upset but you can't blame every bloke you come in contact for your brother's disappearance.

Old man rifles through Rahmo's shoulder bag.

Man- La! No! No please!

Old man- Something you missed U.N?

U.N and Old man check his contents Maria sits in a corner clutching her brother's watch.

Man- No! Do…Do not take my bag…no!

U.N- We're just checking for I.D mate, nothing to worry about, just relax.

Old man pulls out a hand full of watches and gold chains.

U.N- What the f…?

Old man- Souvenirs boy? Hm?

U.N- What do you mean?

Old man- I know what these are U.N! Souvenirs Rahmo? Yes?

Man- Jebi Se! Allaenat ealayk! Do not take my bag!

U.N- Souvenirs? What do mean souvenirs?!

Old man steps on his leg. Rahmo screams.

Old man- Taken from the dead, boy? That what you did?

The U.N pulls him away.

U.N- Leave him! What the hell do you think you're doing?!

Man- Bastard! Allaenat ealayk!

Old man- These are taken from the dead U.N! That's how 'looting' works yes?! This bastard probably stole them once they lay dead am I right?! Am I right boy?!

Old man stamps on Rahmo's leg again and the U.N shoves him away.

U.N- Stop it! How could you possibly know that?

Old man- (*Old man pulls his sleeve up to reveal a tattooed number on his underarm*) because I've seen it! I tell you he took these from the dead, probably from those camps.

Nurse- What camps?

U.N- Detaining camps.

Old man- Death camps! He's Bosniak, yes? He probably got these from Hrasnica or Celebici! I've heard about them. I've heard they're run by cruel bastards.

Nurse- Death camps? Oh God no is that true?

U.N- No it’s not true! Just more of his bloody paranoid gossip! They’re holding camps, detaining camps, that’s all.

Old man- You know what goes on inside those barracks, boy.

U.N- Oh come on there isn’t any evidence to suggest that! Just rumours that’s all! Death camps are extinct, the Geneva Convention prohibits it! So don’t go putting faith into such rubbish.

Old man chuckles in disbelief, he then dumps all the watches and gold chains into the U.Ns hands.

Old man- Prohibits? Prohibits you say? Well there is your evidence U.N! There is your proof! Each one soaked in blood! Maybe you should put more faith in your eyes than your Geneva Convention huh?!

Nurse- Could…could Tomas be in one of those camps?

U.N- No I…I don’t know.

Nurse- Rahmo? Please, I'm begging you, where is my brother is. (*She shows her photograph*) He's a medic in the Territorial Army. He's only a boy! Please, have you seen him?!

Man doesn't answer.

Nurse- (*To the U.N*) Please help me.

U.N- I'll try but you need to calm down.

He gently escorts away from Rahmo.

U.N- Rahmo I need you to listen to me kid. I need to know where you got this watch. It's important! I'm not interested in the rest of your swag, I just need to know about this. Tell me.

Man- I f…found it.

Old man- You found them all boy huh?!

U.N- Quiet!

Rahmo grunts in pain.

U.N- Look Rahmo, I suggest you do yourself a favour mate and tell us the truth. Otherwise we'll find out when we get back.

Man- Jebi se U.N!

U.N- What did he say?

Old man- 'Go fuck yourself'.

Nurse- Please Rahmo!

Old man- Try the Serbs! They'd cut him in ways that would make him talk! Or why not take him to meet your mother girl, huh? She would get her answers like that! (*He claps his hands*)

Nurse- (*Softly*) Please Rahmo?

U.N- I won't ask again kid. Vitez will be full of Croats when we get back, I'm sure they'll be happy to help.

Nurse- (*Desperately*) Please.

She holds the photo to his face.

Man- (*He stares at Maria*) I…I did see him…

Nurse- You did?! Where? Where did you see him?

Man- Celebici…some days ago. I was a 'nothing' a simple munazzaf, a cleaner… But…I was made to do other things.

U.N- Like what?

Man- Digging, burying…getting rid of shit. Dirty job! Shit job! Made me sick! Th…then I was made to bury the dead…

Old man- (*Whispering into his ear*) told you U.N.

Man- First it was the sick, dead from disease. Then it was those who tried to escape, punishment…then…

U.N- …then?

Man- Then it was those killed for fun. That was just the men the women and children had it much worse. Ethnic cleansing is growing. Wiping out the young is essential now. We will not let the future live.

U.N- (*To himself*) Jesus Christ.

Man- Everyone knows what goes on in those camps.

U.N- *(Quietly to himself walking away)* I can't believe what I'm hearing. Just can't fucking believe it! (*Pulls himself together*) how did you get all this gear?

Man- They didn't need them anymore. I took what I could and ran. I wanted to get out I wanted money, I HATE this place! I hate my home! My country! I hope it all burns!

Nurse- (*Exhausted*)…my brother?! Where's my Tomas?

Man- He…h…he tried to escape.

Nurse- …what…

Man- They thought he was a spy…like all men in Bosnia, they are not to be trusted (pause)…I remember him.

Nurse- ...d…dead?

Man- (*Pause*) yes. Along with Sarajevo.

Maria crumples.

U.N- (*Still in disbelief)* you little bastard.

Man- Idi u pakao! I was doing my part! Why don't you take your tanks to Celebici and do yours!

He gasps in pain.

Man- …I could…mushhhka…anymore…I…

He blacks out. A stunned silence fills the room.

Old man- So…what do you want to do?

U.N, still in shock, doesn't answer.

Old man- U.N?

U.N- What?

Old man- What do we do with him?

U.N- I wished I left him in the road. (*Composes himself*) We'll take him back…let the Hague deal with him.

Old man- You are in charge boy.

U.N- I can't believe a kid of his age could… (*still in shock*) Jesus Christ.

Old man- This is war U.N, the world has gone to hell.

U.N- Maria…I'm so very sorry. If there's anything…

Nurse- There's nothing.

She puts on her brothers watch and sits in a corner and closes her eyes. The old man takes his jacket off and wraps it around her. The radio screeches to life and a faint voice is heard.

V.O- **…Alpha…Alpha Four…This is…One…(***Static***)**

U.N- Alpha One-Zero this is Alpha four can you hear me? Over?

Radio crackles.

U.N- Shit! I've gotta get a clearer signal! This could be our rescue! I'll be back!

Old man- Go, go.

U.N leaves.

Old man- (*To himself*) What a fucking day. There's nothing that you or I can say that will bring your brother back. You have my sympathies.

He wanders around and places the watches and gold chains back in Rahmo's shoulder bag. He kneels next to Rahmo.

Old man- You brainless boy. How could you think you could escape hell with a sack full of rings? You'll never escape Bosnia boy, believe me I've tried. You are as damned as the rest of us. These belong with their owners. I'm going to give them back.

He leaves. Rahmo briefly comes around and mumbles incoherently. Maria stares at him from a distance. Distant explosions continue.

Man- Mama…Mummm…I don't…Where am…

Nurse- So you remember him? Moj brat?

Rahmo continues to mumble faintly.

Nurse- And you buried him? You, a child put him in the ground. (*Wipes her eyes*) It's strange…I should feel strong hatred and disgust for you…but even as I look at you now…the only feeling I have…is pity.

Rahmo groans then slips into unconsciousness again, Maria crawls over and sits next to his head and talks to him while gently stroking his head.

Nurse- Poor Rahmo. You poor poor boy. I wish I could understand. How can a boy do such things? What kind of Mother would allow her son to grow into such a monster? When did you realise you were capable of this Rahmo? God help me I'll never ever understand how such cruelty can be endured.

To stomach it so easily! How can God allow it? But then war isn't declared in the name of God is it? It's all man entirely. Why? Why me? What have I done to deserve this? I have done you no wrong and this is what I am given in return…how can this be? Am I missing something? I don't want to know what you did. I don't want to know how many you buried or how old they were my thoughts are already horrified! Why me? I no longer have a family because of you. You...a boy...a kid an infant son of a whore have snatched it away from me! And for what? For what Rahmo?! All my life I've been good, tried to be fair and forgiving and this is my reward? How? How can this be?! Because of you and your brothers, because of your kind you have taken every ounce of hope away from me! You murderer! (Slaps him) You pig! (*Slaps him*) You monster! (*Pulls his hair in anger*) You bastard! How could you?! Why?! If you can take a life so easily…so can I. Maybe it's easier than it looks.

She covers his mouth with one hand and pinches his nose with the other, he struggles and dies. She lays his head down in peace. Old man enters with dirty hands.

Old man- Now the dead can have their belongings in paradise. Christ! Listen to me 'paradise'! Maybe someone can convert in times of stress? Maybe this what you believers mean when you say 'God works in mysterious way'?

No answer.

Old man- Soon we'll be free from this dungeon. Soon we'll be home with our… (*Pause*) I am truly sorry for your loss. Truly. Maybe it's better if you flee this shit country. Never look back. Make new brothers. Maybe our U.N friend will take you home with him? (*Looking at Rahmo*) and you boy, maybe one day you'll teach the world a lesson.

The Old man soon realises Rahmo is not breathing.

Old man- …boy? Boy?!

The Old man shakes the boy.

Nurse- A life for a life.

Old man- (*Pause*) What?

Nurse- A life for a life.

Old man- What do you mean? What have you…?

Looks at Rahmo.

Old man- Oh girl what have you done?

Nurse- (*To herself*) God forgive me.

Old man- What did you do?!

Nurse- I had to do it.

Old Man- …oh no!

Nurse- '*Then the LORD saw that the wickedness of man was great in the earth, and* (*Old man turns and slaps her*)…"

Old man- You dumb bitch! You dumb fucking Croat!

Nurse- (*Silencing him with her scream*) What was I supposed to do? My brother's killer lay at my feet and I'm supposed to help him?

Old man- Girl you…

Nurse- The bible says an eye for...

Old man- You made a decision like that because of some fucking book?! You stupid…

Nurse- You have Gideon lying at your feet, you know what he is and what he's done. What would you do? Let him go? Mend his wounds and send him on his way? Or as you say 'put him out of his misery'?

Old man- Gideon got what he deserved, he betrayed us!

Nurse- Take a look at me! I was betrayed! I had everything ripped away from me (*Softly*) '*An eye for an eye*'.

Old man- But you're only a child.

Nurse- So was my Tomas. You look at me now, you look at me and tell this boy was fit to live after what he did! You tell me, you tell me! (*The Old man doesn't answer*) You cannot, you cannot and you know you cannot.

Old man- After this…you are no different than he was.

U.N enters.

U.N- Bastards! Fuck it! (*Composes himself*) The convoy is here.

Old man- But that is good yes?

Pause.

U.N- I have my orders to take out the seriously wounded…

Old man- We know that U.N!

U.N- …only.

Old Man- What…what do you…?

U.N- The trucks are already packed.

Old man- So? What are you saying?

U.N- I can't…I can't take you. I can only take the wounded. I'm sorry. You have to make your own way to Vitez. (*Pause*) I'm so sorry, I tried to reason with them I tried everything! I begged them! I'm so sorry.

Rumbling from tanks and gunfire from outside.

Nurse- What's that?

U.N- Croats have entered the city. Everyone has to leave now!

Nurse- But you said they were upholding a ceasefire.

U.N- Croats agreed to it just so they could reclaim the town without any casualties. Any non-Croatans found in the area are in serious trouble.

Old man- …like me?

U.N- Look, I've had a thought, if you stay close to the convoy, I could keep an eye on you and…

Old man- I can't run alongside a truck U.N!

Nurse- What if we stay here? Could you come back for us?

U.N- It could be weeks before we come back, I can't make that promise. If you were to hide you might…

Old man- And I am not going to hide like some animal boy! I've done that before. Let luck decide.

U.N- Jesus, I'm so sorry. I begged! I begged them to reconsider! But there are rules. I couldn't do anymore. I'm only allowed to take him. (*Nurse and Old man exchange a look. U.N becomes frantically desperate*) Here! Take all my cigarettes and my whiskey! Take my money! Take it all! Use them to barter, you do that here! They'll get you somewhere safe I'm sure of it!

Nurse- I could speak for you?

U.N- You can! Yes you can! Maria you're Croatian you're safe here! You can talk you can negotiate! You could vouch for him!

Old man- I'm in no mood for talking with liars…or murderers.

U.N- No please you must listen to me! Please I'm begging you! Let Maria talk for you! She won't let anything happen to you. She's the kindest woman I've met. Please! You can do this! She'll look after you. Won't you Maria?! Rahmo! Rahmo wake up mate you're on your way out of here. Rahmo come on! Rahmo wake up please!

He gently shakes him.

U.N- Stop messing around Rahmo! Come on get up!

He puts his head to Rahmo's chest ...nothing.

U.N- Oh no...oh god no! Rahmo! Oh come on son!

U.N begins to pump on the Rahmo's chest counting to himself then blowing in his mouth.

U.N- Come on! (*Pause*) please, please! Don't just fucking sit there! Help me!

Continues to perform CPR.

U.N- Oh come on! Come on son! Please Rahmo! Jesus Christ no, please!

Old man- He's gone U.N let him be.

U.N- No! (*Whispering to himself*) Not this boy. Please God not this boy.

Old man- Boy, let him go! He's dead. Nothing you can do.

U.N stops and hangs his head.

U.N- Give me a fucking break!

V/O- **'Alpha four? This is Major Lewis! Are you receiving over?'**

U.N doesn't answer.

V/O- **'...Alpha four are you receiving? This is Major Lewis, over.**

U.N- (*Composes himself*) Major Lewis, this is Alpha four go ahead, over.

V/O- **'...You have to meet me at your previous location now in order to achieve extraction, over.'**

U.N- (*To himself*) I can't do this. Please God don't make me do this.

V/O- **'...Alpha Four did you copy? Acknowledge, over?'**

U.N- Major Lewis, can an exception be made on transporting two able bodied refugees, over?

V/O- **'...Orders are not to transport any refugees at this time. Wounded civilians and U.N personnel only, no refugees, over.'**

U.N- Christ! Major Lewis, my wounded has recently passed away. Could we substitute his place for a live civilian? They could even take my place? Over.

V/O- **'...Alpha Four, this is no time for sentiments this comes from the Colonel! You have five minutes Alpha Four, out.**

U.N- I tried. (*In pain*) God help me I tried! Please forgive me I tried…

Old man- Boy, you can try and try but you'll never stop hatred like this. I've seen it many times and it never stops burning. War can make the purest angel into a monster (*looks at Maria*). Revenge boy, revenge is too blinding.

U.N- (*Looking at Rahmo*) God help me I didn't want this. I didn't want to leave a failure.

Old Man- When you leave my country boy, don't think of it as a failure, think of it as a lesson, as a warning.

U.N- I'll leave and never give this place a minute's thought.

Old man- ...then I’ll see you again U.N.

Radio screeches to life.

V/O- **‘...Alpha Four…this is Major Lewis…we’re ready to leave…you must leave your current location and meet me now! Over!’**

U.N- Major Lewis, Alpha Four, I’m on my way, out.

He indicates for Maria to leave.

U.N- What’s your name?

Old man- What difference would it make?

Cheering voices and distant gunfire in the distance. U.N leaves. After a moment Maria leaves. The old man follows them to the door way and watches the convoy pull away. Suddenly the radio comes to life, the old man heads over and sits next to it. Another angelic tune plays as all hell is breaking loose outside. The Old Man clutches his radio and shuts his eyes.

Black out.

SCRIPTS FROM APS BOOKS
(www.andrewsparke.com)

Michael Harvey *A Shattered Rose*
Michel Henri *Twenty Pieces Of Silver*
Antony Jenkins *Four Lambs Of Ahmici*
John Wright *Sixteen Screenplays*

www.ingramcontent.com/pod-product-compliance
Ingram Content Group UK Ltd.
Pitfield, Milton Keynes, MK11 3LW, UK
UKHW021925190726
13853UKWH00002B/847

9 798201 026738